1

Table of Contents

To You,

The one I will always love!

LOVE is the mystery of the world,

Nobody has the correct answers

So, stop searching for them

First and foremost, my spiritual guide, my higher power, the one that gives me the talent and the empowerment to survive. Second, my daughter KayCee for her love, support, and generosity of leading me through life. Third, my two sons, Mitch and Hayden, I love you both and you will never know how much you inspire me to just get out of bed every day. Fourth, my daughter Natasha and my granddaughter MicKenna, we might not be together in person but you two are my guiding light in the darkest hour. And for my daughter, November, the days are hard watching your siblings grow each day knowing I will never have those moments with you, even though it's been forever since I laid you to rest, you are never far from my mind and never far from my heart. Lastly, my mother, father, step-father, and my "adopted" parents, Momma Sue and Papa Vaughn, without each one of you I would not be here today writing these poems. Mom, I miss you and I wish you were here to celebrate my achievements with me. Dad, I am finally at peace with you and I love you. My step-father, you have guided me through your wisdom and through your love for me. Momma Sue, thank you for always being there and telling me how proud you are of me and for all the long talks and laughter we have shared. I will forever treasure them. Papa Vaughn, thank you for always being patient while Momma Sue and I tied up the phone with all of our long talks, and for the love, you showed me and my kids.

Note from Poet

 After taking the last year off due to family issues and watching my first granddaughter be born into this world has only given me the time I really needed to decide on where I wanted to go with my career as a poet. I was so unsure and self-doubted myself before. I was unwilling to learn how to be the best I could be and I was unwillingly and stubborn to see that with this self-doubt that it was just hurting me not anyone else. I was awakened to the possibility that I was still only hurting myself for not writing. So, no this is not the book I intended to come back on the scene with, instead it's a collection of love poetry that I have written from three different previous books; Poems, Dreams & More, Poetry Is…??? And Phraseology of Love. The book I wanted to come back to the scene of being a poet is still in the making.

 Being off the screen for so long also gave me the chance to realize what type of poet I am and one I wanted to become. I had the desire, the passion and the craze for love poetry and poetry about life. Unlike many other poets who write about world events and current news that flood our screens of our phones and television, I prefer to write about what life is truly about and that is love. Nothing is grander than love but also at the same time, it fades us away behind locked chains around our hearts when we have been hurt. This book represents me as a poet, a mother and a woman who has been hurt more than once. These poems come from my heart through the experiences I had with my divorce,

Many of these poems, if not all, were written for that secret love that ended by fading away on a starry night a few years ago. I was crushed, devastated and beyond grief when I lost his friendship. The poem, "The Disease" was written after I finally was able to let go but still realized that he had feelings but was too scared to show me. The poem, "Saw You Today" was written after one of our short conversations, again the feelings we had were more than alive, but to no avail would he love me like I loved him.

I hope you enjoy reading these poems and please leave a review!

Beauty

Beauty lies within the soul

Out of sight, but within reach

To grasp a rose, so gentle and delicate

Only in return to be pricked by the thorn

Tears will fall

But the beauty still lies within the soul

For her to shine, in her own way and time

To grasp a hand of a friend, so caringly and loving

Only in return to be pricked by the thorn

Once again tears may fall of sadness,
But the beauty still lies within the soul
Stronger and delicately soft

Only love will find her true
The beauty that lies within her soul.

Arrow

Broken hearts

Never mends

It never heals

Nor never forgets

The pain, the agony

Of the emotional pain

We try to bury it

But it is always there

Like a reflection

Looking in a mirror

A little of me

And a little of you

For this arrow in my heart.

It's You

It's you

You are the one

The one I would

Give the universe too

I would give you all the stars

And the moon too

With the warmth of the sunshine shining

Down onto your beautiful face

It's you

You're are the one

The one I would

Take the bullet for

I would die for you

To breathe

My last breath

It's you

You're the one

The one I would....die for!

Blinded by Your Love

As she sits here, in another heartbroken moment

You cross her mind, till she is blinded by your love

A love that is delicate

As the rose, in a summer field

She waits for your call, to call her back home

To be beside you, in all the miles of a heartache

To subside, like the waves of the sea

She waits, and you never call

Every minute that goes by, her heart is heavy with
sadness

Sadness as in death

Delicate love, like a rose

Needing air to breathe

Every minute without you

Seems like an eternity.

Devotion of Love

I dream of you

I see your eyes

I see your smile

I hear your laughter

I feel your touch upon my skin

I taste your sweet lips

In a dream that won't ever end.

Passion, Caress

Swarming my head

My heart races, my body shivers

All I want is your devotion

Our souls wrap as one,

As I wake, I am alone

Until we meet again in

In a dream that won't end.

Do We Stand a Chance?

Do we stand a chance?

To dance

In life

To touch

Galaxy of stars

Dance among the daisy fields

Feel the sun's rays

Upon our faces

Do we stand a chance?

To sing, the mighty song

In life

To feel stage fright

Brace our weeping souls

Do we stand a chance?

To wed

On this stormy night

As seamen hit the ocean strongly

To sing the mighty song

Galaxy of stars

Dancing

Twirling among

The mighty King

Do we stand a chance?

To have just one more

Sweet, tender, kiss

Tugging at our hearts

As we loved once

Can we love again?

Do we stand a chance?

Crazy About You

When she thinks about you

Her mind begins to spin

Her heart races and butterflies are in her tummy

She thinks of you every day and night

Cannot seem to get you out of her mind

When she closes her eyes

She sees your smile

She can feel your kiss upon her cheek

When she lays herself down to sleep each night

It feels as if she is haunted by your touch

Since the day she met you on that summer day

Wherever she may go, she sees your car

You play the leading roles in the movies

She watches late at night

She gets this feeling deep inside

That she needs to scream your name

So she can just hear it being said

Instead, she walks these beaches alone

Wishing you were there beside her

She sits and plays her favorite songs

Dreaming of dancing the night away

Within your arms so tight

In a moonlight sitting looking at the stars

She wishes upon each night

She wishes that you were hers to keep

From this moment on...

Dreams

I went to the beach, just to take a walk

To clear my mind, of troubled thoughts of you

I sat and waited for you to show

Hoping just for a second, you would get my note

I couldn't get you out of my mind

Not for even for a second of time

I kept the thoughts of you close to my heart

I was wishing that you would have showed

I wanted to tell you how I felt

I wanted to say how I needed you so

And how I lay awake late at night

With my lonely heart wanting you next to me

Wanting to feel wrapped up in my arms so tight

But as I sit and wait, feelings come over me

That just maybe it is just me, and I am just living a dream.

In the Midnight Hour

Sunshine in the summertime

Flip flops and shorts, with a drink in my hand

I hear the music of the band

My toes are tapping to the beat

My head is spinning, as the world flashes by

I hear YOUR voice, I look around

You come to me, so full of grace

With a smile on YOUR face

In the heat of the night, YOU take my hand

We stroll along hand in hand, in the midnight hour

With a flower in my hair and sand between my toes

YOU embrace me with YOUR love and promise me

That YOU will never let go.

The Ride

Jump in

Let's go for the ride

Of our life

Hold on tight

Here we go

Only minutes to go

From here to there

Twisting and turning

Falling and screaming

Down we go

To the bottom

And back up

Hold my hand

Close your eyes

Scream into the night

Now open your eyes

And what do you feel

This is the ride

When YOU fall in love!

Kiss Me

Kiss me in the rain, is what I said

Hold me tight and never let me go

Hug me as if you are hugging the moon

Dance with me, as if you have never danced before

Kiss me in the rain, is what I said

Stand beside me, and hold my hand

Dream with me, not without me

Cherish the little moments, and forget the bad

I know I am not perfect

But I have the will to give

All the love to you

I just want somebody that is true and honest

I want that love that will never die

And never to turn cold on a hot summer night

Kiss me in the rain, is what I said

Wipe my tears away; tell me everything will be okay

When I fall, be there to hold out your hand

Or give me the wings I need to soar

Give me the moon and the stars

But always remember to

Tell ME every day that you love me so.

Magic, Mystic, Moonlight

Magic in the moonlight

Many nights of mystic thoughts of you

May my dreams of you

Come true in the moonlight hour

Magic fills my soul

Mystic flows through my heart

Moonlight has brought you to me

On this magic, mystic, moonlight night

You are the magic which makes our love grow

Always mystical, never a mystery

Dancing in the moonlight

So full of magic, so tender and sweet

Mystic in the way you kiss me.

Love

Love, what is it? Is it a feeling of emotion?

Or is it just a thing that

Brings us joy

Then leaves us broken hearted

Can we measure it? Or see it, touch it?

Taste it, see it upon our faces?

Such as a baby needing a mother's kiss

How can we tell if we are really loved? By the ones we love the most

Or is it all a game

A game that is played

Until our hearts are twine

As one, until the end of time

Breaks the heart

Sends it falling, crashing into hell

Is that what being in love is all about? Is it all a dangerous game?

Of stealing the souls of everyone we meet

Or can love last forever

Full of happiness and tears of joy

You tell me which love

We are headed for

Are we going to play the game?

Or is our love what we make it be.

Just My Love

My love for you enter twines
Like a vine

That slowly creeps
Roots as deep

As roses bloom
There is no doom

Love forever seeks
A peek

In your heart
Shot of a dart

It enters so deep
That love is the only keep

Reminisce

Sweetness is a kiss....

From you to me....

Only to miss

A day without to be....

Loving you is a bliss

May our hearts to see

The reminisce

Of years to the past and to be

The future is ours to this....

Sweetness is a kiss.

Someday

Wanting him, loving him

But he just walks away

As if he is blind to see me

Hugging him, kissing him

Her arms and lips crave to feel his skin

As the darkness rolls in

Her heart is to bleed of tears

Knowing him, seeing him

With her by his side at night

Her soul aches in the coldness

As she lies here all alone

Wanting him, loving him

Hugging him, kissing him

Knowing him, seeing him

She knows someday

She will be his only one.

The Hunt

Love is real, Love is hunger

Hunger for passion, like a lion on the prowl

Longing for what can be found, in the thrill of the
hunt

The lingering thrill of the chase, getting closer to the
kill

Needing to feed the emptiness in the soul, the hunger,
the pain

The eagerness to feel the rush of the kill

To taste the sweetness in my mouth, to feel it upon
my skin

To hear him scream my name in vain, to feel the fire
within our souls

Not knowing when to stop the game, not wanting it to
end

As the dawn breaks, the thrill of the hunt is gone

I awake all alone as if the hunt was real

But within my dying soul, I still taste the sweetness in
my mouth

As the angels call from up above, I know someday
I'll be the chosen one.

The Thief

He strolled into town

On a stormy night

With a curse in his heart

He was to set doom upon

A young lady's heart

He knew his pick, the one he wanted

He had to taste her lips

Feel her breath upon his skin

The curse was eating his soul

Wanting her so much

He dashed his charm

With his crooked grin

Silver-blue eyes gripping her heart

His curse was set

When she said, "I love you,"

She then awoke the next dawn

To find his curse

For he left like a thief

With her heart in his hand

To Be Yours'

Why is it every time I see you?

I get this feeling inside

That I never felt before

My heart races, my mind loses control

I just want to lay it all out on the line

But I know that I can't have you

So I'll wait in time

I don't even know why I try,

To catch your eye

For you have the one you love

I am not as pretty as a dove

But I still can't help myself

For wanting you so

Every place I go

I only hope, I see more of you

Do I ever cross your mind?

Late at night, when you are all alone

Do you ever dream of me, like I dream of you?

Loving You

I lay awake

And think of you

Trying to picture

Your face

From the last time I saw it

It has been a long time

But you have not left this heart of mine

I lay awake

All I want is to love you

To feel your sweet kiss

In the dawn

And to feel your arms

So tight with strength

Around me at night

I lay awake

And think of you

Wishing I could have found you sooner

Before she took your heart

And shattered it

Because now fear lies in our way.

I lay awake

And think of you

Wishing I had some way to convince you

That I would not be her

That I would take your heart

And keep it safe

And love it forever

I lay awake

Knowing this will never happen

So I drift off to sleep for you

To appear in my dreams

Where I know I can

Continue to love you….

Dreams about You

I dream of you

Your sweet smile

The voice I hear

In this mind of mine

Wakes me in the middle of the night

Only to fight to go back to sleep

To see just what happens in these dreams

Just to see if I ever win your love

The lust between two souls

The sweet caress of you touching me

Or do I lose?

Like I feel in the morning light

After this dream has faded

So does your face

But your voice still lingers

In this mind all day long

And well into the night

Only to see your face

Once again appear before

In a dream that never ends

And of course, I continuously lose

For I am still sitting here

Writing these poems

About you and I

In my dreams at night

Chance

I gave you chance

But you said

Friendship only

But why?

I know

You care...

Chances come and go

Passes you by

While standing still

But my feelings

Follows your every step

Why not just leap

And see what

Falls from the stars

It could be great

You and I

I KNOW Who You Are

I know who you are

You haunt my dreams at night

I can see your face slowly fade

I can feel your lips touch mine

I can feel you reaching for me as you fall

I wake up in terror

With chills all over my body

I know your face and who you are

But I want to know is why

You haunt my dreams at night

I know we have met before

I know I am something special

Because you haunt my dreams at night

I feel as if I am falling in love with you

You are on my mind and in my heart

Every moment I breathe

I can see your face

I can feel your touch

Whenever I think about that kiss

As if you were sending me a message

In my dreams; of what it is supposed to be

I don't know

But, I know who you are

Saw You Today

Saw you today,

As you walked closer

I could see the smile

That haunts me at night

I was longing to hear your voice

And there it was

You standing there

Telling me all your great stories

Laughing like we use to

Sharing something special

That we only know is there

Pride is dangerous and cruel

It slips in just in time

Wakes you up and then

There you go

Leaving me standing

There watching you

Walking away

Wanting to run after you

But too scared to

Because all I can feel is

This void that you leave

Within me each time I

See you

But I can smile knowing that

I saw you today.

Just You

Just you are all

I need

Like the air, I breathe

And sunshine

On a hot summer day

Your love is

A blossom of warmth

To my heart

With your beauty

Of a smile

Is all I need to see?

To find my way

Home in the dark

Just you are all

I need

Nothing more

Or

Nothing less

Just you

And

Your love for me

Butterfly Kisses

Soft butterfly kisses

Upon her cheek

Glisten in her eyes

When she looks up at you

She knows she has love

With you

The one for her

Sweet tender butterfly kisses

Upon her lips

She draws you in

To her magic spell

Of love so true

That ties one to another

Soft butterfly kisses….

The Haunt

Taking a drive with you

On hot summer day

Watching you chase

Those butterflies

For me

Dancing underneath the stars

You pulling me close

Wanting more than I dare to show

Only to hear you say

Take me, here and now

Making love under the stars

That night

Will be the event of my life

Only for it all to disappear

For I am already taken

And this was just a dream

Another one of you

Haunting my soul…

The Disease

I was the disease that you never wanted

I played games with your heart

Whenever you looked into my eyes

You couldn't handle the rush of emotions

The feeling of falling

Not knowing if I would be there to pick you up

You played the role of gun and bullet

Out to kill the disease that was aching at your heart

Knowing that the disease is what you wanted

But the pride is the bigger enemy to love

Love would mean letting go

Twirling out of control

The shivers and shakes

The withdrawals

The heartbreaking when you weren't with me

Was all but the disease eating at you?

And you turned your back

Walked away and killed the disease

With the bullet with words of lies

Because I was the disease you wanted all along.

May Not Have You

I may not have you

In face of reality

And you may have told me

That you can't love me

Reality is too hard for you

To face your feelings

That lies at your heart

You choose to fake it

When we both know

That is our dreams at night

You are the only right

For me, I have you there

Where you say all the right things

Do all the right moves

Holding me tight

As to never letting me go

You may have control
Of your love in reality
But I have control
Of it all in my dreams.

Mending

Mending my broken heart

One thread at a time

Don't know how far

I will make it, without you as mine

One thread snap today

When I saw your face the same way

Staring back at me

The vivid ghost haunts my soul to be

Never to be loved, or held again

The dreams begin

And never end

Mending this broken heart

One thread at a time.

Unknown to Me

You are unknown to me

The one I seek and search

For in my dreams

The one that will love me

Hold me tight

On rainy nights

The one that holds my hand

And wipes the tears away

You are unknown to me

But as I continue my search

You lay heavy upon my heart

As you can see

You were the soul mate for me.

The War

The war is raging on

I am not done

Our love is not gone

Like the rising sun

A soldier marching

Into death to fight

For the mighty king

You are my light

Of my life

The one I want

There be no strife

Only nonchalant

Let this war die

Let the wedding bells ring

In heavens high.

For the mighty king

Has won

Your love for me

Like the rising sun

You hold the key

To our hearts

To be as one

Let us not depart

Before we are done….

Mountain Spring

So beautiful and gentle

Tinkling down

So amble

Moving forth, as to drown

My wailing cry

Of a broken heart

Please do not deny

As we depart

From this earth

And to reign in heaven

That our love was worth

And we were chosen

To love not deceit

Angel sings of

Music

So sweet, like doves

Symbol our love

So beautiful and gentle

Tinkling down
So amble…

Moving forth, as to drown
Their cries, of bells to ring
To hear such a sound
At the mountain spring.

Moss

When I woke

This chilly morning

My heart broke

As if your memory was clinging

Like the moss on a tree

One without the other

Is not a norm

As if they were meant to be

We would also be, not norm

In the midst

Of this storm

Of your memory, leaving me a midst

Like a vessel, out on the open sea

Fighting the powerful waves

Such baggage is only a plea

As life tries to save me

Without you
There is no saving
A love so true
So why should I keep begging

As if I was a flower
Begging for sunlight
In the early spring hour
Only to be left at night

All alone, cold and dark
Crying tears
Shedding pain and embarks
A whole new fear

Of loving someone new
Only means to move on from the past,
The heartache
As happiness is drawn.

My Love for You

Sometimes a friendship dies

Because of words that were said

Or is it because of the lies

You said

To yourself, to make you believe

To break the bond

Of two, as you leave

As the day has dawned

One comes to the path

Of life, to decide

To leave the wrath

And to let love subside

Only to feel regret

For years

Knowing that we have met

Only helps the tears

To surface upon your face
As they laid me to rest
In God's grace
You confessed your love

Even though I cannot hear
I always knew you did
To me, there was no fear
Or regret my love for you.

The Battle

Sitting here wishing for the unknown,

Fighting this battle between my heart and mind

Knowing the truth

But trying to fight the ride

Of pain crashing in

Like waves crashing on a beach

Slowly decaying away my love for you

While I sit and wait for my vessel

To come and carry me away

And knowing I will never have you

Fighting this battle

Wanting to beg for your love

But my pride

Is bigger than the waves

Now the time has come

I am sailing my ship

Towards the high seas

Hoping to never see you again

But loving you just the same

As the day
We met...

 This battle continues to rage in my heart
My mind overcomes with darting thoughts
Of you and I
Only to be brought to reality
When my vessel sails away
I would rather fight the wind and rain
Then fight the battle of us back home

Whenever I think of us
As this vessel carries me
Away from you
My heart is still yours
Forever...just as lonely...
When I was with you as if
I never really had you.

You

Why do you do what you do?

Knowing just when to show

That smile, that drives me crazy

The way you flirt, the shine in your eyes

When you look at me

Always knowing how to capture

My heart and hold it there and

Then throw it away while you walk away

With a smile on your face

You know how much I want and need you

You know that it kills me to be so close

And not being able to reach out and touch you

Like I feel the want too

You know that when you leave my heart shatters

And all I want to do is run after you

But instead, I sit and wait

Maybe a few days will past

And I can finally let you go

And get on with my life

But as soon as I let down my guard

There you are, standing there with that smile...

Epilogue

The illusion of poetry displays a view from the poet's eyes on how tragic love can be. But also the tender, sweet compassionate side of love when both parties explore the emotions tied up in the whirlpool of love. As I sat and wrote these poems it was just that, an illusion, playing with my heart as I found out that my marriage had failed and that the love I thought I had for someone so dear to me was nothing more than just an illusion that I felt. Love can be a tricky substance that we all get addicted to at one time or another. I am almost positive this will not be my only book of love poetry from the illusion side of it. I am still young enough to find what love really is and have it there in abundant form but for now, all I still see is the illusion of it all. I must say for the lucky ones that have the real thing, hold it, grasp it and cherish it and never let go. I will continue to wait my turn in line for it to appear until then and until we meet again; I signed off with a huge sigh and laughter for all this is, is an ILLUSION OF LOVE.

26140512R00037

Printed in Great Britain
by Amazon